Small Practices

A Guide to Painless Financial Management & Job Costing

RIBA Publications

Published by RIBA Publications, Construction House, 56-64 Leonard Street, London, EC2A 4LT

ISBN 1 85946 081 X

Product Code 20999

Publisher: Mark Lane

Commissioning Editor: Matthew Thompson

Editor: Ramona Khambatta

Technical Editor: Chris Pomroy (of Smith & Williamson Chartered Accountants, London)

Cover Illustration: Louis Hellman

Design by Red Hot Media, Suffolk

Printed and bound by Dennis Barber Graphics & Print, Suffolk

Acknowledgements:
Sarah Lupton and Chris Pomroy

Contents

Introduction

Mention the word 'money' to most practitioners and the response is that everyone wants it! When it comes to managing money, however, and terms such as 'financial management', 'financial control' and 'financial accounting' are mentioned, eyes glaze over, the little grey cells are switched off and such a task is perhaps left until later in the day.

Obviously, money is important for any business, whether small, medium or large. Taking time to read this guide will not make you a financial expert (and it is always advisable to seek the help of a professional accountant) but it will hopefully ease practitioners into this area by understanding the fundamentals of 'financial management'.

This guide should be used only as a general introduction to financial management and job costing, and is not intended as a comprehensive book on the subject. The text is restricted to an outline of the core accounting concepts needed by a small practice to grasp a basic understanding. These concepts are set out in a straightforward way, avoiding jargon and hence the need for technical knowledge.

A Guide to Painless Financial Management & Job Costing aims to explain the vital role of accounting in the management of an efficient and solvent practice. An architect is in business not solely to earn profits but rather to give the best possible service to his or her clients and, at the same time, to remain solvent, as otherwise he or she cannot fulfil their duty to their clients and staff. To achieve this, it is necessary to programme the work and to keep control over the costs and 'profitability' of the office. Another important financial aspect of a practice is its 'liquid position': a practice cannot afford to expand, however profitable it may appear on paper, if its 'profits' are not available in the form of cash needed to pay salaries, office rent and other expenses which have to be met before clients can be charged any fees.

Four basic tools of financial management are needed to control the profitability of a small practice:

- up to date financial records capable of showing the profitability or otherwise of the practice as a whole;
- adequate costing records reflecting the profitability of individual jobs;
- sound estimates of the future profitability of the practice as a whole, and of individual jobs in hand; and
- reliable forecasts of the likely cash position at dates when it is known that substantial payments will have to be made.

With off-the-shelf computer packages and the ease with which such packages can be incorporated into a small practice for very little outlay, practitioners are able to keep up to date and handle day-to-day financial accounts. There are a number of packages now on the market and it is important to shop around to find the right one for your practice. Talk to your accountant or other small practices, either in your region or further afield, to see what systems they are using – perhaps even ask them for a demonstration. Above all, have a clear idea of what you want the computer package to do for you. If you choose wisely at the outset it will pay for itself in no time at all.

Of course, you may prefer the manual method of pen and paper for managing your finances. Whatever method you decide to use make sure that your accountant approves the procedures you have chosen to follow.

> The prime requisite of any sound system of management accounting is that the basic records must be both simple and up to date.

Accounting terms

Following are the main accounting terms that the practitioner will come across on a regular basis. It is worthwhile spending a couple of minutes just familiarising yourself with these terms as they will appear throughout this Guide.

Accruals

Payments made after a benefit has been received, for example an electricity bill that is paid at the end of a quarter is payment for the electricity used during that quarter.

Assets

These are split into two types:

- fixed assets – those assets that are expected to be held for several years, ie land, buildings, equipment, investments;
- current assets – those assets that are the business resources which would normally be converted into cash within a year as a result of the day-to-day operations of the firm, ie debtors, pre-payments, cash and work in progress.

Cash

Cash can mean cash in hand, the bank balance, uncleared deposits and uncleared cheques.

Costs

Direct costs are those directly related to providing the service and can vary according to the level of turnover and the business generated, eg salaries of fee-earning staff, costs of drawing materials, and any sub-consultants or sub-contractors engaged to help supply services. Indirect costs are the practice's *operating expenses* (see below).

Creditors

A creditor is an entity that has provided goods or services to a firm in exchange for future reimbursement, ie cash.

Debtors

Clients who have not yet paid for services purchased from the practice.

Funds

Either cash and cash-equivalent items, ie an item on the balance sheet representing the cash actually in hand on deposit that belongs to the practice, or working capital, ie current assets minus current liabilities.

Gross profit

The gross profit is the difference between net sales and direct costs or cost of goods sold. The gross profit percentage (gross profit/turnover) is one ratio used to measure performance.

Liabilities

Debts such as claims by creditors. Current liabilities are expected to be met and satisfied within one year, ie trade creditors, tax bills, and bank overdrafts payable on demand. The business may also have long-term liabilities such as bank loans and hire purchase agreements.

Net profit

In a company, the net profit is expressed after the application of interest and provision for corporation tax, neither of which is an operating expense. Interest payable relates more to how the company has financed its operations, whereas taxation constitutes an appropriation of funds.

Operating expenses

The costs of running the business on a day-to-day basis, not the costs directly associated with providing the service, ie rent, rates, light, heat, water, insurance, salaries, promotion.

Operating profit

Operating profit = gross profit – operating expenses.

Partners' drawings

The amounts partners have drawn for their personal expenditure on account of profits generated during the year.

Pre-payments

These are advance payments of expenses, ie insurance or rent which relate to future periods. They are considered assets because they represent 'probable future benefits'.

Reserves

These are also known as retained profits and are arrived at after provision has been made for dividends, ie the distribution of corporate profits, after taxation, to the owners. Profits that are not distributed by way of dividend are retained by the company for further investment.

Revenues and expenses

Revenues are typically earned by providing services to clients. Expenses are costs incurred by the practice in the process of generating those revenues.

Turnover

The total cash and credit sales made during an accounting period. It does not include the proceeds from selling a fixed asset, ie a building, interest from deposit accounts or VAT. The 'net sales' figure does not mean that the practice received the stated figure during the period: it simply reflects those sales that have been invoiced.

Working capital

Working capital = current assets – current liabilities.

Work in progress (WIP)

This is equivalent to the 'stock' in many manufacturing companies, and represents, at cost, the value of doing the work or giving the service that has not yet been invoiced to a client. Such a value is arrived at by adding up the total salary costs of producing the work along with the overheads associated with that work, but it excludes profit on transactions.

Managing practice finances

Accountants provide the essential financial accounting services that every business requires but continuing financial information will also be needed to allow the firm's management to forecast, plan and make decisions. The provision of such information is the function of management accounting, and a primary decision to be made is who in the practice is to be responsible for producing it.

The senior (or sole) partner of a small practice will probably manage its finances, with or without human or electronic help in-house.

The development of standard accounting software has enabled businesses of all shapes and sizes to handle day-to-day book-keeping efficiently and to analyse and extrapolate financial information for the purposes of management and decision-making. However, it is important that architects recognise their limitations in this area and ensure that the practice's book-keeping system and accounting procedures are soundly based and appropriate, and are approved by the practice's accountant.

Profitability is not simply a matter of 'doing well' in the long term or achieving an increase in turnover: it should be seen as a quantifiable target for the performance of the business overall, as a target for each job in its own right and for each fee-earning person employed by the practice.

In times of high inflation a practice that is breaking even on paper is, in real terms, operating at a loss; it follows that setting a level of overall profitability that relates realistically to the economic climate can be a matter of survival. In more stable market conditions, profitability is something that a practice might feel able to take a view about, in line with its character and philosophy.

The question of profit arises whenever a job opportunity materialises. On some jobs costs can be reliably quantified and a profit margin set with confidence; others are less easy to evaluate. Sometimes it might be worth doing a Job X and keeping the profit margin low because there is a good prospect of more work coming in from the client. It is questionable whether it is ever worthwhile taking on a job where it seems that the best outcome will be to break even – and in a period of high inflation, even more doubtful.

Profits can be eaten away by sloppy commissioning procedures. The income expected from each project should be established in the terms of the commission agreed with the client and described in a properly formulated written agreement. If the client subsequently asks for additional services, the client must pay for them: the commission must not be allowed to 'creep' into something more than what was defined in the agreement. Profits are also dissipated by underestimating the time needed to complete the job, and by allocating too much, or inappropriate, staff effort to it.

When assigning staff to projects a balance often has to be struck between skills, availability and costs. On some jobs, the first question to ask might be who is the best project architect for this particular job; on another, who can the practice afford to put on it; or as in the case of most small practices, simply who is available at the moment? If the answer is no one, then the question is whether someone should be brought in on contract.

Setting realistic profit margins depends on a precise knowledge of costs – the cost of running the practice overall; the cost of running each job; and the chargeable and actual cost of each of the people employed by the practice. Previous experience of a particular type of job will help to indicate what level of profit can be targeted but even where the situation is unknown a figure should still be set and job costs meticulously recorded.

Some jobs will be found to be less profitable than others and the reasons for this should be analysed. In some cases it may be the type of work involved, in others it may be the quality of the project team deployed – and there may be other reasons. It is important to read the signs and learn the lessons during a project as well as after its completion; if an unprofitable situation is revealed whilst a job is in progress it may be possible to take corrective action.

The varied and fluctuating nature of commissions does not permit architects to set a once and for all pattern of costing that will assure profitability. Even if the arithmetic is sound, there is always the variability of human factors – key staff may leave or fall ill; there may be a disagreement on policy between partners; or a misunderstanding may arise with the client.

> Watchful and responsible management, supported and implemented by sound technical and financial procedures, will always be needed.

At various times a practice needs to be able to communicate to its investors, creditors, advisers and managers information about its profitability, liquidity, financial viability and the soundness of its business strategy. The function of accountancy is to generate and present this information in a suitable form.

Day-to-day accounting procedures allow the activities of an enterprise to be compiled, recorded and analysed. Transactions are identified, measured in monetary terms, classified and entered in a book-keeping system. They are subsequently summarised in financial statements presented in a form appropriate to the needs of the user. The process of financial management is illustrated later on in this Guide.

Financial statements are used by the Government in the shape of the Inland Revenue (for income and corporation tax purposes) and Customs & Excise (for VAT). Company accounts are filed at Companies House, where they are available to the public. Otherwise, the users of financial statements fall into three major categories:

- investors;
- creditors;
- managers.

Architects could find their accounts reviewed by all three categories.

Investors are those who have a financial stake in the business while creditors may be suppliers of goods who extend credit, or lending institutions such as banks. In addition, there are those who advise the business or have a direct interest in it, eg staff, unions. Practice managers also use financial statements, together with various other reports compiled specifically for management purposes.

The different users of financial statements evaluate the information presented according to their particular needs. Investors or owners are primarily interested in trying to predict a return on their investment and in assessing the risks involved in that investment. They will concentrate on evaluating the firm's past performance and estimating its future profitability and overall financial strength. They will compare it with their investments.

A creditor's primary concern is that the business should be able to repay its obligations (a concern that an architect might have when considering a potential client's financial status). Long-term creditors are therefore concerned with the practice's long-term financial performance and strength; short-term creditors are more concerned with the solvency of the business in the near future and tend to focus on its immediate liquidity.

The key factor in the analysis of financial information is comparability, as unless the present performance of the business can be compared with previous years, or with the results of similar enterprises, or with budget, a financial statement by itself is of limited informational value. Comparing results from previous years may reveal trends and provide a yardstick for evaluating current performance and financial strength.

It is important to establish that the accounting policies and methods used remain constant over the relevant periods.

In accountancy, as in all professions, certain principles and conventions have been drawn up to establish norms and a consistent basis for operation. Accountants conduct their work in accordance with Financial Reporting Standards (FRS).

Principles

There are four principles that need to be understood by anyone attempting to interpret financial statements:

A going concern

Valuation is always based on the assumption that the firm is going to continue indefinitely. An entirely different valuation would be made of a practice's resources and position if its break-up value was being assessed.

Consistency

The same accounting methods are used each year and throughout each year. Any change in this respect has to be stated in the accounts and may require restatement of the previous year's figures.

Prudence

Accountants are often accused of taking a depressing view of events but in financial statements they are required to exercise caution and restraint in calculating profits in order not to mislead the users of these statements. This means providing for losses when they are foreseen and not taking profits until actually made.

Matching

The fundamental principle of accounting is to match expenses against revenues. Thus if a cost occurs in one year, but the revenue does not materialise until the next year, the cost is 'carried forward' and shown in the next year's accounts.

Book-keeping is the basis of financial accounting. The book-keeping system records details of all the firm's business transactions. It contains the information needed for the annual audit where applicable and for preparing interim statements of the practice's financial state of affairs. Its records are the raw material of long-term financial accounting, as well as the information needed to provide up to date statements for management accounting purposes.

It is important to make sure that the system is adequate and appropriate to the needs of the practice, that it works well and that it is being properly operated. It should be regularly reviewed by your accountant.

The double entry system

The double entry system, which is widely used, allows the current financial position of a business to be seen as well as details of its past performance. Its name derives from its basic principle of operation: that every transaction has two opposite aspects of *value received* and *value given*. Therefore each transaction is recorded twice over:

- the account that received value is *debited;*
- the account that gives value is *credited.*

For example, if A charges a fee of £100 to B for professional services rendered then B becomes a debtor (ie he in indebted) to A for £100, whereas A has given value to B in the form of professional services worth £100. Therefore, in A's book it would be recorded that the personal account of B would be *debited* with £100, and the fees account of A would be *credited* with £100.

Balancing the total value received against the total value given reveals the overall financial equilibrium of the business at any time. The statement that results is called a trial balance. If all entries have been posted correctly it will add up to zero.

Double entry system records

Two groups of books are kept:

- books of prime entry;
- ledgers.

Books of prime entry

So called as they are the books in which transactions are first entered.

- Cash book: a record of all transactions with the bank.
- Petty cash book: a record of cash payments.
- Suppliers' day book: a record of suppliers' invoices not for immediate settlement (those for immediate settlement are recorded in the cash book or petty cash book).
- Clients' day book/computerised accounting system: a record of fee accounts sent to clients.

Supporting vouchers are filed and serially numbered according to the books in which the original entries were made.

Ledgers

Items from the books of prime entry are transferred or 'posted' to the various ledgers.

- Creditors' (or suppliers) ledger: a record of 'personal' accounts with suppliers, showing what is payable (ie what the firm owes).
- Clients' ledger: a record of 'personal' accounts with clients, showing what is receivable (ie what others owe the firm).
- General (or nominal) ledger: an analysis of various types of income and expenditure, shown under different headings (eg rent, rates, electricity, etc).

In addition to these books, supplementary documents such as payrolls and time and expenses sheets are necessary, but they do not form part of the 'balancing books' kept under the double entry system. Using a computerised system will mean that an entry only has to be made once. The system automatically posts the opposite entry. A computerised system will also enable the business to generate additional management information from one set of data input.

The trial balance

If the books have been correctly entered it should be possible at any time to draw up a trial balance, consisting of the balance taken from the general ledger.

The ledger is balanced by adding up the debit side balances of the assets type, plus expenditure, and subtracting the credit side balances of the liabilities type, plus income. The total of all balances should be zero.

DEBIT		CREDIT
Assets + expenditure	=	Liabilities + income

From the trial balance, a balance sheet and a profit and loss account can be prepared.

A summary of book-keeping duties

Book-keeping duties are carried out daily, weekly, monthly, quarterly and annually, and can be summarised as follows:

Daily

Deal with banking, petty cash.
Deal with items received in the mail.
Make appropriate entries in double entry system or computerised system.
Raise invoices.

Weekly

Verify the situation at the bank.
Review petty cash activities.

Monthly

Send out fee accounts.
Prepare wages and/or send out salary notifications.
Deal with PAYE adjustments.
Settle month end accounts.
Pay office bills.
Compile, record and pay staff expenses.
Prepare financial statements as required for management accounting purposes. These might include:

- cash flows;
- profit and loss matched against budget and last year;
- fees outstanding and amounts owing;
- bank reconciliation.

Quarterly

Prepare VAT return.

Annually

Prepare for annual audit by accountant.
Put away the year's files and prepare new ones.
Compare profit and loss with annual budget.

Petty cash book: suggested headings

Cleaning
Repairs and renewals
Postage
Stationery
General expenses
Drawing materials
Photographs
Technical library
Fares and subsistence
Car expenses
Entertainment

Standardised formats for financial accounting reports have been developed by the accounting profession. A set of statements for an accounting entity would cover:

- its financial position at the end of a period (the balance sheet);
- its revenue and expenses for the same period (the profit and loss account);
- its investments by, and distribution to, owners during that period;
- its flow of funds for the period;
- its statement of accounting policies;
- its auditors' report, if applicable.

The two key statements are the balance sheet and the profit and loss account.

Balance sheet

Sparrow & Grebe Ltd: balance sheet as at 31 December 1999

	£000s	£000s
FIXED ASSETS		
Land and buildings		100.0
Office equipment		60.0
		160.0
CURRENT ASSETS		
Stock, & work in progress	20.0	
Debtors	140.0	
Cash at bank	40.0	
	200.0	
Less		
CURRENT LIABILITIES		
(due within 1 year)		
Creditors	60.0	
		140.0
Net Current Assets		300.0
Less		
LONG-TERM LIABILITIES		
(due after 1 year)		
Bank loan		100.0
		200.0
CAPITAL RESERVES		
Share capital		60.0
Reserves		140.0
		200.0

Prepared February 2000

The balance sheet shows the financial position of a firm at a given point in time.

It is made up of assets, liabilities, capital and reserves.

Assets

Assets are used to help generate, either directly or indirectly, future revenue for the firm. They can be tangible (fixed), like buildings and equipment, or current, such as money owed to the firm or work in progress. However, to be included in the balance sheet the value of every asset must be measurable in monetary terms.

Liabilities

Liabilities are debts, ie what the firm owes. They are claims by the creditors on the firm's assets. A creditor is someone who has provided an asset to a firm in exchange for future reimbursement, usually in the form of cash. Trade creditors in the balance sheet represent the amount owed to suppliers of goods and services. Other liabilities will be to the Inland Revenue, and will include bank loans and/or overdrafts.

Liabilities are split into current and long-term. Current are expected to be met and satisfied within one year; long-term after one year.

Capital and reserves

In a partnership this will be represented by the partners' capital account, which shows the profits distributed to them from the P&L account, less any withdrawals (drawings) that have been made. In a company's balance sheet this would be reflected in two principal items: share capital and reserves.

Profit and loss account

Sparrow & Grebe Ltd: profit and loss (P&L) account for year ending 31 December 1999

		£000s
Sales		640.0
Less: Cost of Sales		347.0
	Gross Profit	293.0
Administrative expenses		192.2
	Operating Profit	100.8
Bank loan interest payable		23.8
	Net Profit before Tax	77.0
Tax		25.0
	Profit for Year	52.0
Dividends payable		30.0
		22.0
Plus: Reserves b/f		118.0
Reserves c/f		140.0

Prepared February 2000

The profit and loss account shows the firm's revenue and expenditure over a period. In the case of a company the P&L account will also show the amount of profit that is re-invested in the company, the dividends that are paid to shareholders, the accumulated net profits from the previous year's trading, and the tax liabilities. In the case of a partnership, it will illustrate the amount of profit that remains to be allocated to each of the partners.

The P&L account enables a firm's past financial performance to be evaluated. Whereas the balance sheet reflects its financial position at a point in time, the P&L account shows the in-flows and out-flows of resources over a period, expressed as revenues and expenses.

In architectural practice, revenues are earned by providing services to clients. Expenses are costs incurred by the practice in the process of generating those revenues. All the revenues and all the expenses are added up to show the net result of the practice's operations over a period, ie its profit.

Published P&L accounts usually add all the operating expenses together, whereas those accounts used for internal management purposes analyse the operating expenses in greater detail under a range of budget headings, for example:

Profit & loss account: management accounts

Sparrow & Grebe Ltd: profit and loss account for year ending 31 December 1999

	£000s	£000s
Income		
Fee		640.0
Other		nil
Total		640.0
Direct costs		
Technical salaries	(297.0)	
Consultants' fees	(25.0)	
Other expenses	(25.0)	(347.0)
GROSS PROFIT		293.0
Premises expenses		
Rent, rates, insurance	42.0	
Utilities	11.0	
Repair and renewal	5.0	(58.0)
Administrative expenses		
Staff salaries	52.1	
Staff training	4.5	
Staff pensions	4.2	
Motor expenses	12.4	
Depreciation	16.6	
Printing, stationery	7.0	(96.8)
Financial expenses		
PI insurance	20.0	
Professional advisers	10.0	
Bank charges	3.2	
Bad debts	4.2	(51.4)
TOTAL EXPENSES		192.2
OPERATING PROFIT		100.8
Less: Bank loan interest payable		(23.8)
Net profit		77.0

Prepared February 2000

Management accounts comprise the information provided by the ledgers and cash book presented in a way that enables decisions to be made about practice planning and operation. Their presentation and timing are determined by the needs of the practice and will relate to its size and the nature of its work. The function of the management accountant is to interpret and extrapolate information to monitor and control the direction and profitability of practice finances. The main aspects of his or her work are budgeting, and financial control – in other words:

- where the practice is going;
- how to keep it on course.

Some architects are reluctant to attempt any form of budgeting ahead, whether for the office as a whole or for individual jobs, for two main reasons:

1. *The impossibility of predicting what new work will come into the office during the coming year and therefore what the total income will be.* This precarious nature of the architect's inflow of work is a problem that may call for variations in the orthodox management accounting procedures as applied to other professions or to commerce. However, far from removing the need to budget, it makes it even more necessary to make a realistic appraisal at the beginning of the year of what the financial position of the office will be for the year ahead if no new work should come in.

2. *The difficulty of forecasting how much time a particular job will require and of controlling the time spent on a job as it goes through.* This difficulty is at least capable of control to the extent that it is always possible, when working for a predetermined fee, to calculate how much time can be afforded on a particular job if it is not to be carried out at a loss. This then provides the basis against which to measure the time actually spent at different stages, so that steps can be taken to correct in advance a developing unprofitable situation or, if this cannot be avoided, to use the experience gained when planning future work.

As a first step, therefore, it is essential to prepare, before the beginning of each financial year, forecasts of aggregate income and expenditure, based on the most realistic appreciation of the situation as known at that particular time.

It is used to set targets for the level of fee income anticipated, staff salaries and other direct costs, logistical support, office overheads, and, ultimately, profit for the year. It indicates how much money can be made available for marketing, training, new systems, furniture, equipment, books, etc.

The annual budget consists of a series of agreed budget headings (see over).

Annual budget: budgeted P&L account

Sparrow & Grebe Ltd: 2000 annual budget

	£000s	£000s
Income		
Fee		600.1
Other		2.9
Total		603.0
Direct costs		
Technical salaries	(260.0)	
Consultants' fees	(20.0)	
Other expenses	(20.0)	
GROSS PROFIT		303.0
Premises expenses		
Rent, rates, insurance	42.0	
Utilities	12.0	
Repair and renewal	6.0	
Administrative expenses		
Staff salaries	50.8	
Staff training	9.0	
Staff pensions	4.0	
Motor expenses	12.4	
Depreciation	17.6	
Printing, stationery	6.2	
Financial expenses		
PI insurance	21.5	
Professional advisers	10.0	
Bank charges	3.5	
Bad debts	5.0	
TOTAL EXPENSES		200.0
OPERATING PROFIT		103.0
Less: Bank loan interest payable		(23.5)
NET PROFIT BEFORE TAX		79.5
		Prepared December 1999

The amount of budgeted fee income represents the commissions expected to materialise during the year ahead. Direct costs include technical salaries, consultants' fees, drawing office materials and other recoverable expenses. Overheads (indirect costs) include all the costs of running the business that are not directly associated with projects. They typically consist of fixed or recurring charges (many of which are known in advance or can be realistically adjusted), such as rent, rates, utilities. Of the costs remaining, some can be estimated on the basis of previous expenditure, deducting any abnormal items and adding any known additional commitments.

The budget is set once a year, but as mentioned above, the assumptions and forecasts on which it is based may well change in the course of the year, so that at strategic intervals it will be necessary to review and revise the budget to take account of any actual or expected changes.

The annual budget is the key control document for assessing overall profitability and it can be used as the basis for quarterly or monthly analyses of income and expenditure. Any overspending on budget can be identified and corrected; conversely, if budget targets are not met for some particular initiative or commitment (staff training, for example), the reason should be investigated. It is important for accounts staff to be clear about who is responsible for authorising expenditure under the various budget heads, and they in turn should make sure that those with such authority are kept informed of the position each month.

The annual budget for a small practice can be broken down into monthly elements and supported by cash flow forecasts; the larger the practice becomes the more detailed the information, which might include overhead costs analyses, performance indicators, forecast balance sheets and funds flow statements.

A level of overall profit will also be budgeted. A primary decision is how much is to be retained in the business as working capital and how much is to be distributed to partners or shareholders.

A crucial aspect of management accounting is financial control – of cash flow, time and costs.

Controlling cash flow

Cash comes in to the firm in several ways, such as:

- payment received against invoices;
- money invested in the firm;
- bank loans;
- proceeds from the sale of the firm's assets.

Cash goes out from the firm (and at times seems to go out very quickly and regularly!), to pay staff, creditors, and to reward partners or shareholders.

The difficulty in architectural business is coping with the time lag between doing the work and being paid for it so as to maintain equilibrium in the bank balance, ie solvency.

How can this situation be managed?

It stands to reason that the best positive action is to be properly funded in the first place and to control the factors that are capable of control, and the best defensive action is to anticipate the worst situation and know what to do if it arises.

Payments out

As far as outgoings are concerned, there are many peaks and troughs of expenditure that can be levelled out. It is often possible to arrange to pay annual bills such as gas and electricity in monthly instalments. Non-urgent orders for books, stationery, drawing office and computer supplies can be placed when the cash is available.

Payments in

Getting the money in is far more difficult. A basic business practice that architects are traditionally diffident about is establishing the creditworthiness of prospective clients. Discreet inquiries of professional contacts are often the most reliable indicator but using a credit reference agency is inexpensive and anonymous and is certainly better than nothing. Checking creditworthiness should be done as a matter of routine with new clients, or where large additional costs are agreed when work is in progress.

There are certain disciplines that will help to get the money in regularly. An important one is to insist that clients pay on a monthly basis. Every appointment should clearly specify the terms of payment, and these should always be recorded in writing. The arrangements agreed should suit the practice's accounting procedures and financial situation as well as the client's convenience.

Unfortunately, in business there are always some consistently late payers and a few never pay at all. Practices need to establish a policy for dealing with both these situations and agree a cut-off point for work in the event of non-payment (say, three months). It is wise to put in place chase-up procedures to deal with late payers so that the problem does not become large-scale; unless the money comes in, the solvency of the practice will be threatened. Repeat work for bad or slow payers should be carefully considered and only undertaken if more effective controls can be put in place – or if the job is priced accordingly.

The cash flow situation

As well as establishing basic controls of this kind, the general cash flow situation should be constantly monitored, and this is done by means of cash flow forecasts (see below). One is usually prepared based on the annual budget to show the likely position at the end of the new accounting year and to serve as a check on the budget, and again at regular intervals throughout the year. It will highlight any surpluses or shortfalls, allowing decisions to be taken about possible investments or whether an additional loan or overdraft will need to be negotiated.

The manager of a small practice might produce a cash flow forecast every three months. They can relate to the practice's running costs and to its expected fee income. These can be combined to give an overall picture of liquidity over the year or be broken down to show the situation over shorter intervals.

Cash flow forecast

Sparrow & Grebe Ltd: 2000 Annual Budget

	Jan-Mar £000s	Apr-Jun £000s	Jul-Sep £000s	Oct-Dec £000s
Receipts				
Fee income	125.0	132.8	181.2	149.3
Other	0.1	1.7	0.3	1.2
	125.1	134.5	181.5	150.5
Payments				
Capital expenditure	nil	nil	(15.6)	(24.2)
Salaries	(72.2)	(72.1)	(84.6)	(95.8)
Fees	(14.7)	(3.2)	(15.3)	(14.9)
Rent & rates	(17.0)	(7.0)	(17.0)	nil
Stationery etc	(2.8)	(1.0)	(3.0)	(1.7)
Insurance	nil	(1.5)	(30.0)	nil
Other	(10.4)	(5.7)	(42.0)	(21.9)
	(117.1)	(90.5)	(207.5)	(158.5)
NET CASH MOVEMENT	8.0	44.0	(26.0)	(8.0)
Plus: Opening balance	17.0	25.0	69.0	43.0
Closing balance	25.0	69.0	43.0	35.0

Prepared December 1999

Bracketed figures are outgoings from the bank account.

Architects often have to make fee quotations in competition with others and have to know exactly how low they can bid without sacrificing profits. This means that, whatever the fee basis for a job is, they have to be able to assess and measure with precision its work content and the related staff effort needed to service it. It is essential for financial survival that the price charged for providing the professional service required by the client takes into account all the costs involved, direct and indirect.

The only element of a professional service that can be measured is the time taken to provide it. This has nothing to do with the quality of that service or the competence of the people involved in its provision; these are things that have to be judged and assessed – they cannot be measured. Even where there is a tangible product such as a feasibility study or an investigative report, the client pays for the time taken to produce it, not for the aptness or excellence of its recommendations. The tangible, but 'priceable', commodity of the service that architects provide is *time*.

The direct costs of a job arise from the amount and level of staff effort allocated to it. The time of an experienced job architect is considerably more expensive than that of a student on Professional Training, although both may expend the same amount of time on the same job. Failure to get the experience–inexperience balance right can reduce efficiency and, ultimately, profitability.

When a job comes in, it is necessary to calculate how much staff time will be needed to complete it, and to put a price on that time. The crucial management tool in job costing is the time sheet.

The time of a full-time architect is spent in five principal ways:

- carrying out project work;
- looking for new business;
- management and administration;
- training and development;
- legitimate absence.

Time spent on promotion and advertising would be included under new business, and CPD activities under training and development. Sickness, holidays and other legitimate absences have to be included in the reckoning.

All staff, non-technical as well as technical, should be asked to complete time sheets and hand them in each week. To allow time expenditure to be analysed, time sheets can be divided into the five major time categories described above, with individual projects listed under Project Work and identified by job number and Work Stage where appropriate. It must be made clear to everyone exactly what counts as 'project time', and what is the smallest unit of time that is to be recorded.

Example time sheet

Sparrows & Grebe Ltd Time Sheet		Name:			Week			
		Date completed			Signature			
Projects		Monday	Tuesday	Wednesday	Thursday	Friday	**Total**	**Overtime**
Partner i/c	Job no.	hrs	hrs	hrs	hrs	hrs	hrs	hrs
JR	927	5	3	6			14.0	
CJ	641		2.5		3	6	11.5	
Promotion/ business development					.5	1.0	1.5	
Management/ administration			2	1.5	.5	.5	4.5	
Training/ development		2.5					2.5	
Personal/ absences					3.5		3.5	
TOTAL		7.5	7.5	7.5	7.5	7.5	37.5	

Notes
1 Working day is 7½ hours.
2 Minimun unit time to be recorded is 15 minutes.
3 Overtime work to be agreed beforehand with project partner.
4 For job costing purposes, it is important to take into account agreed overtime rates.

Time spent on project work is directly chargeable to each project, but time under the four other categories is not. The question therefore arises of how the cost of that other time is to be recovered. All the hours in the working day have a price, there is no 'free' time – salaries have to be paid and the costs of running the business have to be met.

Senior staff may spend about half their time on non-chargeable work; partners often as much as 80%, and junior staff only 10-15%.

Analysis of time expenditure by grade of staff

	Projects	Promotion/ business management	Management/ administration	Training/ development	Personal/ adsences
Principal	45	20	25	3	7
Associate	60	10	20	5	5
Senior professional	70	5	15	5	5
Professional	75	nil	10	10	5
Junior professional	85	nil	3	7	5

Notes
1 Read this Figure in conjunction with the example time sheet.
2 The percentages assume a working week of 5 days, and a working day of 7½ hours.

If 70% of a job architect's time is fee-earning, the remaining 30% has to be recovered by the price put on the job. If the ratio of chargeable to non-chargeable time can be improved, profitability should similarly improve. This ratio should be closely watched.

It is never easy to persuade staff of the need to complete time sheets, which is often seen as a tiresome chore imposed on busy people who consider they are already doing their best. Staff are more likely to comply if care is taken to explain why time sheets are needed – particularly if it is pointed out that they are a mechanism used to improve efficiency and profitability, which will bring benefits for the staff themselves.

The time of non-technical staff can sometimes be charged as a direct project cost, such as special research and secretarial back-up, computer time, or information provided by in-house specialists, but more often it cannot and in any case this is a matter that should be agreed with the client. However, it is still important for non-technical staff to complete time sheets as this often provides valuable information about the underlying costs of providing a professional service.

Calculating realistic hourly rates

A small practice will need to identify for each fee-earning member of staff an hourly rate that both recovers all the costs of employing that person and includes a margin for profit. (For a larger practice it may be more appropriate to work out an average rate for each grade of staff.)

The first step is to calculate the number of fee-earning hours available in a year:

Calculating the number of fee-earning hours

Assumptions	A 5-day working week A $7\frac{1}{2}$-hour working day Paid annual leave: 20 days Paid public holidays: 8 days		
			Hours
Total hours	Per year ($52 \times 5 \times 7\frac{1}{2}$)		1,950
	Minus		
	Public holidays ($8 \times 7\frac{1}{2}$)	60	
	Paid holiday ($20 \times 7\frac{1}{2}$)	150	
	Sick leave (say)	40	
		250	250
Fee-earning hours	Number of fee-earning hours per year per full-time member of staff:		1,700

Other information needed is:

- the percentage of fee-earning time given;
- details of staff salaries;
- the direct employment costs of each staff member;
- the practice budget.

The method of calculation is given below:

1	2 Basic salary	3 Other direct empl. Costs	4 Indirect costs	5 Total cost of empl. p.a.	6 Fee earning % of time	7 Fee earning hours	8 Cost per fee earning hour	9 Add 20% margin	10 Fee earning potential p.a.
	£	£	£	£	%	hrs	£	£	£
Principal	40,000	9,000	20,000	69,000	45	765	90	108	82,620
Assoc sen. Profess.	30,000	5,000	20,000	55,000	60	1,020	54	65	66,300
Sen. profess.	25,000	3,000	20,000	48,000	70	1,190	40	48	57,120
Profess.	20,000	2,000	20,000	42,000	75	1,275	33	40	51,000
Jr profess.	15,000	1,000	20,000	36,000	85	1,445	25	30	43,350

Notes

All figures given are purely illustrative and should not be taken as a realistic guide.

Column 3: Direct costs apart from salary include payroll costs, such as bonus, employer's NI contributions, and benefits (car, pension, private health, etc). These will vary with the grade of staff if in a larger practice.

Column 4: Indirect costs ('overheads') include salaries of administrative staff, PI insurance and all costs of running the business that are not specifically project-related. They are divided equally amongst the five categories of staff (see (6) below).

Column 5: Columns 2, 3 and 4 are added together to give column 5.

Column 6: These are assumed fee-earning percentages. In practice, the figure for principals will vary widely, and might be as low as 20% – even lower in some cases. In such cases it might be more realistic to redistribute all or part of principals' non-chargeable time as an overhead (ie included in column 4).

Column 7: The column 6 percentages of assumed total available hours (ie 1,700) are converted into hours.

Column 8: The cost per fee-earning hour is calculated by dividing total employment costs (column 5) by the number of fee-earning hours (column 7).

Column 9: The figures in column 8 with a 20% weighting. Obviously, the appropriate profit margin will vary according to the particular job.

Column 10: The potential fee income for the grade of staff is calculated by multiplying the number of fee-earning hours (column 7) by the profit-weighted hourly rate (column 9).

Taking time sheet data as its base, this approach enables the total cost of employing each member of staff to be seen, the cost of each fee-earning hour and, adding on an appropriate margin, the annual fee-earning potential of each grade/member of staff. The point of the exercise is for architects to be able to know the real costs of employment each time they are required to put a price on a commission so as to be sure that these costs are going to be recovered. The RIBA published fee scales and hourly rates are only indicative and do not remove the need for sound arithmetic based on up to date cost information for each new project.

Typically, the larger a practice becomes, the more time partners need to spend on management and looking for new business, and the less time they spend on direct project work. However, sooner or later the question will arise of how to rationalise in a job costing system the relatively high salary of a partner with the relatively low percentage of his or her time that may be charged directly against the project. It may be more realistic to regard the non-chargeable element of a partner's time as a practice overhead. In the calculation, it would then be absorbed evenly by the other grades and is shown in column 4.

It must be stressed that the method demonstrated is only one way of approaching the arithmetic and it is based on various arbitrary assumptions. It does not take into account the many variations in skill, seniority, efficiency and appetite for work between individual staff. Time spent on a job can be measured but arithmetic says nothing about how effectively that time has been spent. The human factor should not be ignored.

Managing the workload

Calculating the practice's fee-earning potential has an important application as a strategic control in managing the practice's existing and expected workload. This requires a realistic forecast of fee income to be kept under review, so that action to recruit additional design or other staff can be taken as necessary.

The forecast could take the form of a schedule of all committed work, ie all commissioned projects and any prospectives that are judged likely to materialise. The best way to monitor and control variable data of this kind is to use a computer spreadsheet. There are many add-on packages that work in conjunction with accounting software to forecast income on a monthly basis and record fees invoiced and received. In this way a running check can be kept on the status of each project and its performance against target. This allows fine-tuning to be done if a lean period is indicated or a possible overrun means there may be a shortage of key staff to start a new job. If similar information is compiled relating to the actual expenditure of practice overhead costs against budget, a picture of the overall liquidity and profitability of practice finances can be produced.

Speculative work

Carrying out work before a commission has been formalised is obviously risky, although most jobs start off as 'prospectives', to be converted to 'in progress' status when commissioned. In some cases, of course, the project does not proceed and the work done proves abortive. This is of no great consequence if it amounts to a few sketches and the odd meeting, but there must be a defined cut-off point for such 'free' work. Records should be kept of the amount of time spent and at the cut-off point each should be given a prospective job number and budget. It will then at least be possible to assess the cost of the job realistically and, if it proceeds, even to recover the cost of some of the preliminary work.

Job overruns

A soon as a job overruns, its profits begin to be eroded. The reasons for the overrun must be stringently investigated. The fee quotation or time estimate may have been unrealistic, or the balance of staff assigned to the project may have been inappropriate or their performance inadequate. It may be that work additional to the original commission has 'crept' in. Whatever the reason, the lessons must be learned.

Day-to-day control

The practice's bank balance must be kept under constant review, so that credit is not exceeded or unnecessary loans maintained. Surplus funds should not be allowed to lie idle, and automatic transfer into an interest-earning account should be considered. Three monthly reviews are suitable for small practices.

It is essential to know exactly where the money goes. A great deal is often lost by careless administration at a day-to-day level. Book-keeping records should be studied and analysed; they will often reveal where waste is occurring and economies can be made, or where stricter control is needed.

An important management consideration is to identify who is responsible for authorising expenditure. Accounting procedures simply expedite the decisions of others; it must always be absolutely clear where authority for expenditure lies, what limits there are, and to whom the authorising person is accountable.

Accountancy software

There is a wide range of accountancy software, and it is essential that the staff who will be using it have, or acquire, a working knowledge of the basic principles of day-to-day financial accounting, ie book-keeping. Although most accountancy software programs are easy to use, those using them must understand what they are trying to produce and for what purpose. To use computing vernacular, what goes in as garbage will come out as garbage!

The same general caveat applies to all systems, manual or electronic: however sophisticated and time-saving they are, they do not remove the need for sound judgement and thoughtful management.